summersdale

A LITTLE BIT OF OLD GIT WIT

Copyright © Summersdale Publishers Ltd, 2009
With text contributed by Aubrey Malone
All rights reserved.

Summersdale Publishers Ltd
46 West Street
Chichester
West Sussex
PO19 1RP
UK

www.summersdale.com

Printed and bound in Great Britain

ISBN: 978-1-84953-006-4

Substantial discounts on bulk quantities of Summersdale books are available to corporations, professional associations and other organisations. For details telephone Summersdale Publishers on (+44-1243-771107), fax (+44-1243-786300) or email (nicky@summersdale.com).

A LITTLE BIT OF

Old Git Wit

TOM HAY

Contents

Editor's Note

Despite the reading glasses and hearing aids, these veterans' witty comments and acerbic remarks show that at least their sense of humour has remained firmly in place – even if everything else has taken a somewhat saggy journey south. Now you can laugh out loud as age-afflicted academics, writers, politicians, comedians and actors share the trials and tribulations of getting old – some more disgracefully than others!

As Maurice Chevalier so aptly put it, old age is not so bad when you consider the alternative.

Time's Winged Chariot

Unfortunately, it kills all
its students.

Billy Crystal

The older I get, the
older old is.

Tom Baker

Time is the best teacher.
There comes a time in every
woman's life when the only
thing that helps is a glass
of champagne.

Bette Davis

I'm so old that when I get up
in the morning I sound like
I'm making popcorn.

Lawrence Taylor

Don't retouch my wrinkles in the photograph. I would not want it to be thought that I had lived for all these years without having anything to show for it.

The Queen Mother

—◆—

I am now at the age when I
must prove that I'm just as
good as I never was.

Rex Harrison

—◆—

Amazed.

George Burns when asked how he felt getting up in the morning

The only whistles I get these days are from the tea kettle.

Raquel Welch

I'm so wrinkled I can screw my hat on.

Phyllis Diller

One of the many pleasures of
old age is giving things up.

Malcolm Muggeridge

An old man looks permanent,
as if he had been born an
old man.

H. E. Bates

I don't know that my behaviour has improved with age. They just found somebody worse.

Jimmy Connors

From Here to Eternity

All men are cremated equal.

Ben Elton

If they don't have chocolate in heaven I'm not going.

Roseanne Barr

It's a funny old world. A man
is lucky to get out of it alive.

W. C. Fields

For Catholics, death is
a promotion.

Bob Fosse

If people really believe that
death leads to eternal bliss,
why do they wear seatbelts?

Doug Stanhope

This chap told me his wife's an angel. He's lucky – mine's still alive.

Roy 'Chubby' Brown

I believe in life after death, which is strange, because at one time I didn't believe in life after birth.

Ozzy Osbourne

I think the resurrection of the
body, unless much improved
in construction, is a mistake.

Evelyn Underhill

He had decided to live forever
or die in the attempt.

Joseph Heller

❦

I don't believe in afterlife,
although I am bringing a
change of underwear.

Woody Allen

❦

Old florists don't die, they just make other arrangements.

Nigel Rees

Bodily Betrayal

I've started to use my left
breast as a bath plug.

Joan Rivers

The older we get, the better
we used to be.

John McEnroe

———— ❖ ————

I have the body of an 18 year old. I keep it in the fridge.

Spike Milligan

———— ❖ ————

Old people should not eat
health foods. They need all
the preservatives they can get.

Robert Orben

It is obscene to think that
some day one will look like an
old map of France.

Brigitte Bardot

When people tell you how young you look, they are also telling you how old you are.

Cary Grant

… it was taking longer and longer to wash my face.

Harry Hill on the realisation that he was going bald

Old age puts more wrinkles in
our minds than on our faces.

Michel de Montaigne

I have everything I had 20 years ago, only it's all a little bit lower.

Gypsy Rose Lee

… my eyes aren't what they used to be. They used to be my ears.

Spike Milligan

Oh, Bitchery

Every morning I read the
obituary page over breakfast.
If I'm not in it, I get up.

Benjamin Franklin

I've just learned about his illness. Let's hope it's nothing trivial.

Irvin S. Cobb

Pushing 40? She's clinging
onto it for dear life.

Ivy Compton-Burnett

There's nothing wrong with
you that reincarnation
won't cure.

Jack E. Leonard

They say you shouldn't say nothing about the dead unless it's good. He's dead. Good.

Jackie Mabley

I hope *The Times* has my obituary ready because I haven't been feeling very well recently.

Spike Milligan

In Liverpool, the difference
between a funeral and a
wedding is one less drunk.
Paul O'Grady

Ambitions

I wouldn't like to die on stage.
I'd settle for room service and
a couple of dissipated women.

Peter O'Toole

When I die I want… ten per cent of my ashes thrown in my agent's face.

W. C. Fields

I would like to live in
Manchester, England.
The transition between
Manchester and death would
be unnoticeable.

Mark Twain

If I had my life to live over
again, I'd be a plumber.

Albert Einstein

When I die I want everything
to be knackered.

**Hamish Imlach on the
deterioration of the body**

I want to live to be 80 so I can piss more people off.

Charles Bukowski

When I die I want to leave my body to science fiction.

Steven Wright

Grand Lives

My grandmother's 90. She's
dating. He's 93. They never
argue. They can't hear
each other.

Cathy Ladman

My grandmother is 92 years old and she hasn't a single grey hair. She's bald.

Bernard Manning

My grandmother is over 80
and still doesn't need glasses.
Drinks right out of the bottle.

Henry Youngman

Anytime I appear on television my granny turns her hearing aid off.

Julian Clary

What's the difference between an Italian grandmother and an elephant? Twenty pounds and a black dress.

Jim Davidson

My grandfather reached a hundred and was then shot by a jealous husband.

Finlay Currie

Romantic Yearnings

My husband will never chase
another woman. He's too fine,
too decent… too old.

Gracie Allen

I used to demand good looks.
Now all I ask for is a
healthy prostate.

Joan Rivers

I can still enjoy sex at 75. I live at 76, so it's no distance.

Bob Monkhouse

I asked the life insurance man
what I'd get if my husband
died tomorrow. 'About fifteen
years,' he told me.

Bette Davis

Yes, I'm dating again but I can't say any more. We don't want to rush into anything.

George Burns at 93

God's cruel joke: by the time a guy figures out how women work, his penis doesn't.

Adam Carolla

My parents have been married
for 55 years. The secret to
their longevity? Outlasting
your opponent.

Cathy Ladman

The older I get, the more passionate I become about fewer things.

Brendan Kennelly

A Ripe Old Age

We don't grow older, we
grow riper.

Pablo Picasso

I attribute my great age to the simple fact that I was born a very long time ago.

John Gielgud

Youth is a wonderful thing.
What a crime to waste it
on children.

George Bernard Shaw

Beautiful young people are accidents of nature, but beautiful old people are works of art.

Eleanor Roosevelt

―•―

… no more than a bad habit,
which a busy person has no
time to form.

Andre Maurois on growing old

―•―

What's a man's age? He must
hurry more, that's all;
Cram in a day what his youth
took a year to hold.

Robert Browning

God grant me the senility to
forget the people I never liked.

Terry Wogan

Old age is life's parody.

Simone De Beauvoir

God gave us our memories so
that we might have roses
in December.

J. M. Barrie

Autumn is mellower, and what we lose in flowers, we more than gain in fruits.

Samuel Butler

Good cheekbones are the brassiere of old age.

Barbara de Portago

Oh to be 70 again!

**Georges Clemenceau on his 80th
birthday after spotting a
pretty girl**

Don't let ageing get you down. It's too hard to get back up.

John Wagner

Doctor, I'm in Trouble

My doctor told me I had hypochondria. 'Not that as well!' I said.

Kenny Everett

My doctor told me to do
something that puts me
out of breath.

**Jo Brand on taking up smoking
again**

—◆—

The doctor told me I was in good shape for a man of 70.

Les Dawson on being fifty

—◆—

I don't want to put my life in the hands of anyone who believes in reincarnation.

Glenn Super on Indian doctors

For all the advances in
medicine, there is still no cure
for the common birthday.

John Glenn

Doctors are always telling us that drinking shortens your life. Well I've seen more old drunkards than old doctors.

Edward Phillips

I had a cholesterol test. They found bacon.

Bob Zany

‐✦‐

'Doctor, my irregular heartbeat
is bothering me.'
'Don't worry, we'll soon put a
stop to that.'

Fred Metcalf

‐✦‐

Every morning when you're 93, you wake up and say to yourself, 'What – again?'

Ben Travers

Birth Daze

I'm pleading with my wife to have birthdays again. I don't want to grow old alone.

Rodney Dangerfield

Whenever the talk turns to age, I say I am 49 plus VAT.

Lionel Blair

When I was young, I was told: 'You'll see when you're 50.' I'm 50 and I haven't seen a thing.

Erik Satie

Zsa Zsa Gábor has just celebrated the 41st anniversary of her 39th birthday.

Joan Rivers

I tried to count the candles on my birthday cake… the heat kept driving me back.

Bob Hope

I'll never make the mistake of being 70 again.

Casey Stengel

He had too many birthdays.

Andy Marx explaining the cause of his father Groucho's death in 1977

Birthdays only come once a year unless you're Joan Collins, in which case they only come every four years.

Steve Bauer

Passing your 80th birthday is a wonderful achievement. You just sit there and it happens.

Angus McBean

✦

I'm 59 and people call me
middle-aged. How many
118-year-old men do
you know?

Barry Cryer

✦

I believe in loyalty; I think
when a woman reaches an
age she likes she should
stick to it.

Eva Gabor

By the time I lit the last candle
on my birthday cake, the first
one had gone out.

George Burns at 80

I should have suggested a
minute's silence.

**Alan Bennett on how to celebrate
Harold Pinter's fiftieth birthday**

Birthdays are nature's way of
telling us to eat more cake.

Jo Brand

I do wish I could tell you my age but it's impossible. It keeps changing all the time.

Greer Garson

A diplomat is a man who always remembers a woman's birthday but never remembers her age.

Robert Frost

Birthdays are good for you.
Statistics show that the people
who have the most live
the longest.

Father Larry Lorenzoni

Anyone can get old. All you
have to do is live long enough.

Groucho Marx

✦

Age to women is like
Kryptonite to Superman.

Kathy Lette

✦

Musical Cheers

I'm old enough to remember
Elvis the first time he
was alive.

Noel V. Ginnity

Getting old is a fascinating thing. The older you get, the older you want to get.

Keith Richards

—◆—

When I was young we didn't have MTV. We had to take drugs and go to concerts.

Steven Pearl

—◆—

She was an ageing singer who
had to take every note above
'A' with her eyebrows.

Montague Glass

People tell me I'm a legend. In other words, a has-been.

Bob Dylan

❧

I guess I don't so much mind
being old, as I mind being fat
and old.

Peter Gabriel

❧

~•~

I was a veteran before I was
a teenager.

Michael Jackson

~•~

The best epitaph for a blues singer would be, 'Didn't Wake Up This Morning'.

Burl Ives

People like their blues
singers dead.

Janis Joplin

Afflictions of Age

I don't deserve this. But I have arthritis and I don't deserve that either.

Jack Benny on receiving an award towards the end of his life

I am getting to an age when
I can only enjoy the last sport
left. It is called hunting for
your spectacles.

Sir Edward Grey

❦

I do, and I hope to have it
replaced very soon.

**Terry Wogan on whether he
knows the meaning of 'hip'**

❦

I advise you to go on living solely to enrage those who are paying your annuities. It is the only pleasure I have left.

François Voltaire

Age is a high price to pay
for maturity.

Tom Stoppard

My knees are on their
last legs.

Paul McGrath

Eventually you will reach a point when you stop lying about your age and start bragging about it.

Will Rogers

Growing old is like being increasingly penalised for a crime you haven't committed.

Anthony Powell

'Do you know who I am?'
'No, but if you go up to the
desk, the matron might be
able to help.'

**Exchange between Gerald Ford
and a patient at an old folks home
where he was making a speech**

—◦—

I wasted time, and now doth
time waste me.

William Shakespeare

—◦—

I've got to the stage where I
need my false teeth and my
hearing aid before I can ask
where I've left my glasses.

Stuart Turner

❖

As you grow old, you lose interest in sex, your friends drift away, and your children often ignore you.

Sir Richard Needham on the *advantages* of ageing

❖

It's not the hearing one
misses, but the overhearing.

David Wright

There is absolutely nothing to be said in favour of growing old. There ought to be legislation against it.

Patrick Moore

Just remember, once you're
over the hill, you begin to
pick up speed.

Charles M. Schulz

Grey hair is God's graffiti.

Bill Cosby

The whiter my hair becomes,
the more ready people are to
believe what I say.

Bertrand Russell

Wrinkles are hereditary. Parents get them from their children.

Doris Day

Checking Out Time

Only the young die good.

Oliver Herford

Immortality is a long shot, I admit. But somebody has to be first.

Bill Cosby

I could never bear to be buried
with people to whom I had
never been introduced.

Norman Parkinson

I am ready to meet my Maker.
Whether my Maker is ready
for the ordeal of meeting me
is another matter.

Winston Churchill

Dying can damage your
health. Every coffin should
contain a Government
Health Warning.

Spike Milligan

Reports of my death are
greatly exaggerated.

Mark Twain

Committing suicide is the last thing I'd ever do.

Kenny Everett

❧—◦—❧

Memorial services are the
cocktail parties of the
geriatric set.

Harold Macmillan

❧—◦—❧

How young can you die of
old age?

Steven Wright

Last month my aunt passed away. She was cremated. We think that's what did it.

Jonathan Katz

You live and learn, then you
die and forget it all.

Noël Coward

The defence rests.

Suggested epitaph for a lawyer

Exit Lines:
Famous Last Words

Either that wallpaper goes
or I do.

Oscar Wilde

Doctor, do you think it could've been the sausage?

Paul Claudel

No flowers please, just caviar.

Jennifer Paterson

Dear Elise, seek younger friends. I am extinct.

George Bernard Shaw

❧

I've just had eighteen
whiskies. I think that's
a record.

Dylan Thomas

❧

If this is dying, I don't think much of it.

Lytton Strachey

Last Will and Testament: I,
being of sound mind, have
spent every penny.

Ray Ellington

━━●◆●━━

This is no time for making
new enemies.

**Voltaire after being asked
to renounce the devil on his
deathbed**

━━●◆●━━

All in all, I'd rather be in
Philadelphia.

W. C. Fields

✦

They couldn't hit an elephant
at this dist-

General John Sedgwick

✦

Don't let it end like this. Tell them I said something.

Pancho Villa

Have you enjoyed this book? If so, why not write a review on your favourite website?

Thanks very much for buying this Summersdale book.

www.summersdale.com